Sight Words

BreAnna –
I hope you are
encouraged
by these words.

[signature]

MARV LOUCKS

ISBN 978-1-63575-688-3 (Paperback)
ISBN 978-1-63575-689-0 (Digital)

Christian Faith Publishing, Inc.
296 Chestnut Street
Meadville, PA 16335
www.christianfaithpublishing.com

Printed in the United States of America

There are words that most of us learn at a very early age. These are known as sight words. They are the approximately two hundred words that are the most frequently used words in the English language. Children learn sight words, so they will know them instantaneously. Sight words are essential for building fluency.

There is another group of words that should also be considered sight words—powerful, meaningful words that you should never let out of your sight. Words that can put you in a position to win in life. But these words by themselves will not bring you success. You have to own them and live by them.

The Rotary Club I am a member of distributes dictionaries to every third grader in our community. A few years ago, I noticed these words that a teacher had written on the whiteboard in one of the classrooms. It read, "Own Your Words." I thought immediately of a book I read several years ago written by Duke Basketball Coach Mike Krzyzewski titled *Beyond Basketball: Key Words for Success.* It is a book, not about basketball, but about words. For Coach K, as he is known, certain words have special importance. There are about forty words in his book, words he uses to teach and motivate. Words like *adaptability, adversity, communication, excellence, poise,* and *selflessness.*

The dictionary, Krzyzewski said, is a great place to study and learn words, but you are only borrowing them. This book, like Coach Krzyzewski's, is not about borrowing words. It is about *owning* them.

In this book, I have listed one hundred words that I once only borrowed. Now, I own them. These are important words. These are words have changed me and made me who I am today. I believe they can alter the course of your life also and put you in position to be successful in life. Take it from me. Let me save you some frustration and heartache. Heed these one hundred words.

What is the significance of one hundred words? It is a round number and seems to fit. When a new president is sworn into office, it is common practice to evaluate the new administration's first one hundred days.

The first one hundred days can be important for individuals, families, and businesses too. They can set the tone for the rest of your life. *Sight Words* is a short read, but I hope the power of each word will be long lasting.

Here is what others have to say about the power of words:

> *"Words are singularly the most powerful force available to humanity. We can choose to use this force constructively with words of encouragement, or destructively using words of despair. Words have energy and power with the ability to help, to heal, to hinder, to hurt, to harm, to humiliate and to humble." (Yehudi Berg)*

> *"Words—as innocent and powerless as they are, as standing in a dictionary, how potent for good and evil they become in the hands of one who knows how to combine them." (Nathaniel Hawthorne)*

> *"As we express our gratitude, we must never forget that the highest appreciation is not to utter words, but to live by them." (John F. Kennedy)*

> *"Words have a strong impact in our lives—you have the power to speak encouragement or persecution over others." (The Jubilee Project)*

You might have a word that is personal to you. A word your parents or grandparents or a teacher or coach have shared with you. Or a word you have discovered on your own. Words will change your life. They can change your family tree.

Let's take a look at some sight words.

Attitude

Opinion or feeling; posture

I did not choose to begin this list with *attitude* because it begins with the letter *A*. I chose to make it first because it is vital to success in life.

Your attitude is so important that John Maxwell calls it the difference maker. It can be your greatest asset.

"The first rule of winning is don't beat yourself. If your attitude isn't as good as it could be, and you fail to take personal responsibility for it, then you are beating yourself. However, if you look in the mirror and can with honesty say, 'The attitude I possess is my responsibility and no one else's,' then you're on your way."

You are going to meet with discouragement and adversity in your life. You can expect it. So, get your attitude right before it happens.

Let the late Zig Ziglar provide you with a tip: "It's not what happens to you that determines how far you will get in life; it is how you handle what happens to you."

Author and pastor Chuck Swindoll said basically the same thing: "Words can never adequately convey the incredible impact of our attitudes toward life. The longer I live the more convinced I become that life is 10 percent what happens to us and 90 percent how we respond to it."

Olympic skater Scott Hamilton was right when he said, "The only disability in life is a bad attitude."

How is your attitude?

Today's Winning Thought: A negative mind will never give you a positive life.

Adversity

difficulty or misfortune

It is not a question of *if* you face adversity in your life. It is only a question of *when*. You will experience adversity. You do not have to like it, but if you expect it, reframe it, and embrace it, the adversity you face will make you better and stronger.

Adversity does not ask you if there is a convenient time for you. It just interrupts. That is okay. Remember, you were expecting it. If you remain strong, the adversity will be invaluable. Keep battling through it.

You might be going through an intense crisis. If you are, I pray you will come through it. But it is also likely you are just dealing with a common case of everyday reality. If so, take a deep breath, refocus, and keep moving forward.

When adversity comes tomorrow or next week or next month, stare it right in the face. Don't back down.

In his book, *You'll Get Through This*, Max Lucado writes, "You'll get through this. It won't be painless. It won't be quick. But God will use this mess for good. Don't be foolish or naive. But don't despair either. With God's help, you'll get through this."

Today's Winning Thought: What adversity are you currently facing in your life? How are you defeating it?

Advice

opinion urging choice or rejection of a course of action; piece of information

When his son was preparing to head off to college for his freshman year, H. Jackson Browne Jr. went to his family room to write some observations and words of counsel that he believed his son would find useful. Those words of wisdom are compiled in a small booklet titled *Life's Little Instruction Book*. The book has 511 suggestions, observations, and reminders on how to live a great successful life.

I am not a college freshman, and you might not be either. But this book is full of good advice, regardless of our age. In the introduction to the book, Browne wrote that his son called him a few days later. He wrote, "Dad, I've been reading the instruction booklet and I think it is one of the best gifts I have ever received. I am going to add to it and someday give it to my son."

Be careful about who you ask for advice. Make sure it is someone you trust and respect. When you ask for it, consider it carefully. If it is good, you should take it.

Today's Winning Thought: What advice do you need? Don't be afraid to ask.

Appearance

external or physical aspect; presence

Perhaps it is not fair, but people will make a judgment about you based on your appearance. People will notice how you are dressed, how you are groomed, your posture, the shape you are in, how you carry yourself, and how you speak.

Your appearance matters. You are sending a message, whether you know it or not. How are you presenting yourself? You do not have to wear $100 shirts or $1,000 suits, but dress nicely. Buy quality clothing, on sale—always! Price and cost are not the same thing. Quality clothing and products will cost you less in the long run. You will look (and feel) better, and your clothes will last longer.

Consider your shoes, hair, and hands, too.

I used to think this saying was a bit silly and old-fashioned, but it is very true: You only get one opportunity to make a good first impression.

Today's Winning Thought: Take a look at yourself in a full-length mirror. How is your appearance? Every part of it. And your words, how do they sound? They are part of your appearance.

Arrogant

unduly or excessively proud; overbearing; haughty

I could write a list of people who I think are arrogant that would spill over into a dozen pages, but I won't. Who I consider to be arrogant is not important. What is important is that you do not become arrogant.

Arrogance is a real turn-off. No one I know likes to be around that kind of individual. It can create a real disconnect. Arrogant people just suck the air out of a room. Don't be arrogant. It will not gain you many friends.

Today's Winning Thought: There are enough arrogant people in the world. Do not add to the list.

Average

the ordinary rank, degree or amount; general type

Average is ordinary. Don't be average. People do not like to pay for average. They do not want to pay $100 to watch average baseball players on a major league field. They do not want to pay that much to attend a concert with an average singer. Nor do they want to pay hard-earned money for a very average meal.

Former college basketball coach George Raveling once said, "Never ever allow yourself to be 'average' in anything you do. Fight every day of your life against average."

Professional golfers fight every day against being average. Sometimes, a lot better than average still is not even enough. At the 2015 Masters golf tournament, Justin Rose and Phil Mickelson finished second and third respectively. Their scores would have been enough to win most Masters tournaments. But not in 2015. A twenty-one-year-old player, Jordan Spieth, played the tournament of his life and finished three shots better than the two other older veteran players. On this particular week, better than average was not even enough to win golf's biggest prize.

H. Jackson Browne said, "A racehorse that consistently runs just a second faster than another horse is worth millions of dollars more. Be willing to give that extra effort that separates the winner from the one in second place."

Believe this: average will never be good enough. Don't settle for average. You do not want an average surgeon operating on you. Average should not be acceptable in the real world.

Have the attitude of baseball great Joe DiMaggio. "There is always some kid who may be seeing me for the first time. I owe him my best."

Give your best effort. You owe that to yourself and the people you will meet in life.

Today's Winning Thought: What is so special about being average? Nothing.

Adjustments

cause to fit or function properly; settle; adapt oneself

I attended a leadership conference one time and heard the facilitator ask what concerns we had for our organization going forward in the next five years. He asked, "What do you need to adopt, adapt, and abandon?"

So let me ask you: What do *you* need to *adopt*? What do you need to start doing?

What do *you* need to *adapt*? What are you doing that you can improve by making some changes and adjustments?

What do *you* need to *abandon*? What should you stop doing now?

Coaches expect to make adjustments every time their team plays a game. You should expect to have to make adjustments in life, whether you are sixteen or sixty.

CJ Johnson is a young man who served as a counselor at Heather's Camp, a summer camp in the Midwest for young people who are blind or have low vision. CJ is nearly blind himself. But he did not allow his lack of sight to steal his vision. CJ is a certified lifeguard, a certified lifeguard trainer, and an EMT. When I last spoke to him, he was studying to be a paramedic. Do not miss CJ's message. He told a group of us, "The world is not going to adapt to me, so I have to adapt to the world."

Adopt. Adapt. Abandon.

Today's Winning Thought: You should expect to make many adjustments in life.

Believe

to have confidence; have faith

Successful people believe in themselves. And they are careful about who they take advice from. These very successful and well-known people did not listen to the naysayers. Here are some of the things they were told.

Mary Kay Ash's attorney told her to liquidate her business, Mary Kay Cosmetics, and recoup whatever cash she could. If she would not do that, she would end up penniless. I hope she changed attorneys because that one gave her bad advice.

Estee Lauder's accountant said basically the same thing. "You've got no chance of success." Oh, really?

"No market for it. If there were, major airlines would already be offering it." That is what advisors said to Fred Smith, founder of Federal Express.

Harrison Ford, the highest-grossing actor in US box office history, was once told by a studio official, "You'll never make it in this business." Be careful who you listen to and with the information you receive.

And Arnold Schwarzenegger's family once asked him, "How long will you go on training all day in a gymnasium and living in a dream world?" Some dream he had, huh?

You have to believe in yourself because there will be plenty of others who will not. If you do not believe in yourself, how can you expect your employer or coworkers or customer to believe in you?

Today's Winning Thought: Do you believe in yourself? If not, what has to happen in your life to change that?

Basics

most important or significant; essential

If you look closely at championship teams and athletes and the best and most successful companies, you will find that they all have something in common. The best are the best because they do the basic things very, very well. They are fundamentally sound. They have to be.

They also leave nothing to chance. Like legendary football coach Vince Lombardi. It is said of the coach that at the start of summer training camp, he would hold a football above his head and pronounce, "Gentlemen, this is a football." You cannot get any more basic than that.

Mark Batterson, the author of *All In*, wrote, "The concert pianist started with scales. Every PhD went to kindergarten." Pretty basic stuff.

Master the basics. Take nothing for granted. Leave nothing to chance. Nothing!

Today's Winning Thought: It will be hard to succeed in school, sports, business, or life if you cannot or will not do the basic things well.

Bold

have courage; fearless; showing or requiring
courage; daring; confident; assured

What do you want to do with your life? What kind of work have you determined you will do? If you are undecided, how will you choose?

Except for rare cases, you will probably go to work after you complete your education. And in all likelihood, you will work many years. It is pretty important that you have a plan or, better yet, a purpose. At least have some idea.

This idea might give you a jump-start if you are stuck. It might help you find your purpose. Why are you here on earth? What are you passionate about? What burdens you? What bothers you to the point you decide you must take action? What are you doing about it? The answers to those questions might point you in the direction of your calling.

When you know what you want in life, pursue it boldly with all your heart and mind. Be bold. Ask for opportunities. You have to earn your way in this world, nothing will be given to you. Don't expect something for nothing. And you would not want it any other way. But there will be people who will give you an opportunity. Be bold enough to learn and gain skills you will need *when, not if,* your opportunity comes.

Today's Winning Thought: Be strong. Be courageous. Be bold.

Build

to construct, erect or make by assembling separate parts or materials; to establish or increase; to found; make a basis for; to renew or strengthen

Over time, during my sales career, I have been blessed to be able to build a nice account list. I have not done this work alone. It has taken a team.

Building, whether it is a list of customers, a consensus of people, or a building, takes time, and effort. And teamwork.

Building a life takes time too. And you should give careful attention to detail. Do not look for shortcuts. A shortcut will often take you on the longest and most expensive path. You do not want that.

A few years ago, I watched in amazement as construction crews and bricklayers completed a new football stadium in our community. They built it with precision, one brick at a time, one day at a time. That is what it will take in life if you want your life to be a masterpiece.

Today's Winning Thought: What are you building? Do not ignore the first, and perhaps the most important step—a solid foundation.

Courage

that quality of mind or spirit enabling one to meet danger or opposition with fearlessness, calmness and firmness; bravery; heart; spirit; disposition

Joshua was a warrior, a leader, and for forty years served as a special assistant to Moses. Joshua succeeded Moses as Israel's leader. He was prepared to take over, but it would not be without challenges. (Read the story of Joshua in the Old Testament.)

If Joshua was to succeed, God told him he would have to be strong and courageous. He did not tell him once—he said it three times.

You do not succeed and get through trying times simply because you have power or know people. It also requires courage.

Today's Winning Thought: Look life square in the face. Live with courage.

Champion

person who fights on another's behalf; athlete winning or getting first place in a series of competitions; advocate of a cause; defend or advocate

Do you want to be a champion? Here are some characteristics of a champion.

Champions have courage.

Champions have hope.

Champions have great attitudes.

Champions motivate others.

Champions persevere.

Champions have integrity.

Champions nurture their relationships.

The late boxing great Muhammad Ali said, "Champions are not made in the gym; champions are made from something they have deep inside them—a dream, a desire, a vision.

Today's Winning Thought: Play, live, and act like a champion today.

Chaos

utter disorder and confusion

I was following a car one day and noticed a decal on the rear window. It read, *Team Chaos.*

If you have not noticed, life can get pretty chaotic at times. Don't freak out. Try to stay calm.

There is a great book by David Jeremiah titled *Living with Confidence in a Chaotic World.* He writes that there are ten key actions we must take when life gets chaotic.

Stay calm.

Stay compassionate.

Stay constructive.

Stay challenged.

Stay connected.

Stay centered.

Stay confident.

Stay consistent.

Stay committed.

Stay convinced.

Stay. It means to remain or continue.

I would add one more. Stay courageous.

Today's Winning Thought: There will be days, and maybe seasons, when life will get chaotic. Do not be surprised by that.

Character

the combination of qualities or traits that distinguishes an individual or group; any distinguishing attribute; moral force; integrity; reputation

Character matters—a lot. There are countless examples of people—about one per day from the National Football League, it seems—who have ran afoul of the law. Some just did something foolish or stupid. Others simply lack character. Some lost their jobs, some lost money—a lot of money. Others have even lost their life.

I read a tweet shortly before writing about this word. It read: "Talked to a college coach today who pulled four offers from guys who tweeted derogatory comments about women. Think before you tweet."

That affected those players' college careers. The sad part is that it does not have to be that way.

Today's Winning Thought: The great basketball coach John Wooden said, "Be more concerned with your character than your reputation, because your character is what you really are, while your reputation is merely what others think you are."

Commitment

to devote oneself unreservedly; pledge; bind; an
engagement or to pledge to do something

Bill Snyder is a college football coach. When he was named head coach at Kansas State University, that program was, to put it politely, just plain horrible. Under Coach Snyder's leadership, Kansas State became one of the most respected college football programs in America.

Snyder is not just a football coach, he is father figure and a mentor to hundreds of young men. The impact he has had on their lives cannot be measured.

One of the things Snyder's players will remember well, after their playing careers are over is Snyder's 16 Goals for Success. Those goals formed the foundation for the greatest turnarounds in college football history. They will work in any individual, family, classroom, organization, and company in America. Here is Coach Snyder's list:

Commitment.
Unselfishness.
Unity.
Improve.
Be tough.
Self-discipline.
Great effort.
Enthusiasm.
Eliminate mistakes.
Never give up.
Don't accept losing.
No self-limitations.
Expect to win.

Consistency.

Leadership.

Responsibility.

You might have noticed that the list begins with commitment and it ends with responsibility. I hope you will make a commitment to be successful and take personal responsibility for making it happen.

Today's Winning Thought: How committed are you? Committed enough to win?

Counsel

advice given as the result of consultation;
opinion on what to do; guidance

Do not be afraid or hesitant to seek counsel from wise people. People who are successful. People who know you and who you know, trust, and respect. If you are a man and you are married, I would strongly encourage you to ask for and listen to the counsel of your wife. That has been absolutely valuable beyond reckoning to me.

Surround yourself with a network of strong people. Proverbs 15:22 says, "Plans fail for lack of counsel, but with many advisers they succeed." Do not close your mind to new options and ideas.

Today's Winning Thought: Be careful about where you seek counsel.

Communicate

to cause another or others to partake of or share in; impart; to convey knowledge of

I read an article once that listed twenty-five business skills one must master now to be successful. They are not just good for business, they are important for life.

The first skill people must master, according to the article written by Randall Hansen, is communication. You have to be able to communicate in today's world. You cannot communicate too much. And you need to know how.

I know many young people who will not likely reply to your e-mail. And they use their cell phones to text, not talk.

Listening is another skill you must master. I am having a difficult time understanding why it would be listed twenty-third on the list I read. Listening is a huge part of communication.

In his book *3 Seconds*, Les Parrott writes, "Three seconds is enough time to give your first impulse a second thought."

During your next conversation, try this: pause three seconds before you reply or respond. Just take three seconds to formulate what you heard and your response.

Today's Winning Thought: Learn to listen and speak well and to write clearly and concisely.

Confess

admit as true; profess belief in

In his book *Rumsfeld's Rules*, former Secretary of Defense Donald Rumsfeld writes about the advice and life lessons that have served him well during his long career in business and government.

I was barely through the introduction of the book when I noticed this gem. It is great advice if you or someone you know is lost or adrift. Rumsfeld learned this lesson while in naval flight training. "If you are lost," he writes, "climb, conserve, and confess."

Here is what he means.

Climb means that the pilot should gain altitude so that he could see a greater distance, get his bearings, and if necessary, glide without power to a safe landing. *Conserve* means reducing airspeed and "leaning out" the fuel mixture to conserve fuel and have more time to figure out where he is. And *confess* means getting on the radio promptly and announcing to all who might be listening that you are lost and you need help.

Today's Winning Thought: If you have gotten off course, these three words might help you get back on track: Climb. Conserve. Confess.

Composure

apparent calm

I spent many years as a college basketball referee. There are some things I learned about life from officiating.

Composure. Basketball is a fast-paced game. Today's players are bigger and quicker. The game is physical. Coaches are under more pressure. Crowds are boisterous. When things get intense, you have to keep your composure. That works in life, too. Learn how to handle pressure.

Excellence. Officiating is the only business in the world where you have to be perfect to start with and get better as you go. Perfection is not humanly possible, but you should strive for excellence. You are going to miss a call once in a while. You just have to try to keep them to a minimum.

Communicate. You will have many opportunities during a ballgame to communicate with coaches and players. When a coach wants an explanation and is professional, you help yourself by communicating with them. Coaches are going to tell you what they think. As long as they do not cross the line, let them have their say. You do not always have to have the last word.

I heard a veteran official—a man who worked the Final Four—say that you cannot quote silence. That will also help you in life.

Position. I did not need to be the fastest person in the arena. I did need to put myself in a position to succeed. Do the basic things well. Be there mentally. Stay focused on your responsibilities. Be where you are supposed to be. Don't give up. Finish strong.

Timing. You should not look at the game as forty minutes or two twenty-minute halves. Veteran officials and coaches focus from time out to time out. Media timeouts are four minutes apart. Focus on what you have to do and when. Do not get ahead of yourself and rush things. And do not cut corners.

Officials are observed and graded. Every play, every game, even what you do off the court is scrutinized. You will also be observed and graded in life, in your job. Grade high. Pass the test.

Today's Winning Thought: Keep your composure when others around you do not.

Creative

of an original mind; inventive

Moziah Bridges is a teenager. He is not your stereotypical teenager. He does not dress like a normal teenage boy. He has a passion for fashion. He likes to wear bowties because they make him look and feel good.

When Mo was nine years old, he could not find a bowtie that he liked. So he started making his own from his grandmother's scrap material. Eventually, Mo began selling the bowties. Today, he is an entrepreneur. His company, Mo's Bows, has changed his life.

Mo said designing a colorful bowtie is part of his vision to make the world a fun and happier place. Each year, he selects one tie to sell specifically to help send children to summer camps.

As a young boy, Mo saw his mother work hard for someone else. He wanted his own company, and he created it.

Today's Winning Thought: You do not have to take what life gives you. Be creative. Dream a little. Be bold. Be open to the endless possibilities. Work hard.

Death

the permanent cessation of all vital functions in an animal or plant

I do not want to make you uneasy with this word. It is a part of life. I decided to include it on a day that I lost a friend. He was a great guy, and he lived a wonderful life.

Every one of us will die. We are born, we live our lives, and we will die. Author and speaker Darren Hardy said that we are dying every day.

I attended a funeral recently of a man who was sixty-one—my age. As I grow older and attend more funerals, I find myself thinking about the rest of my life. Not the *end* of my life, but the *rest* of it.

Someday, we will all die, of course. But until then, live your life. Make it count. Live with purpose. Live with no regrets.

Today's Winning Thought: Live with a sense of urgency. Do not think you are invincible. Do not waste minutes. Make your life count.

Determined

having or showing fixed purpose; resolute; firm

You might have heard some of these sayings:

"When the going gets tough, the tough get going."

"You are never a loser until you quit trying."

"Failure is not an option."

And this from Calvin Coolidge: "Nothing in the world can take the place of persistence. Talent will not: Nothing is more common than unsuccessful people with talent. Genius will not: Unrewarded genius is almost a proverb. Education will not: The world is full of educated derelicts. Persistence and determination alone are omnipotent."

Simon T. Bailey said losers focus on what they are going *through*. Champions focus on what they are going *to*.

Today's Winning Thought: *"Determination looks for the opportunities. It won't take no for an answer." (H. Dale Burke)*

Decisions

choice or judgment

You will have to make decisions for the rest of your life. Some will be easy and simple. Some will be more complex and difficult. Some of your decisions will impact your future and, perhaps, the rest of your life. Some decisions will also affect other people and maybe for the rest of their lives.

How will you make these decisions? What will guide you? You will likely make them from what you know and from what you believe. If you are wise, you will seek counsel of a parent or someone you trust. But ultimately, the decision will be yours. Think things through carefully, Think with your future in mind.

Today's Winning Thought: Don't be careless with the most important decisions you will have to make.

Discipline

training that develops self-control

I do not make New Year's resolutions. I choose to focus on one word. A few years ago, I chose *discipline* as my one word. I selected that word because everything I wanted to improve about my life could have been fixed with a little more self-discipline.

It has been said that the difference between ordinary and extraordinary is that *little extra*. This book, and my first one, would have been published much sooner than they were if I had exercised a little extra discipline. But I got a little lazy and lost my focus and drifted occasionally.

Olympians do not do that. World-class athletes and the greatest musicians cannot allow themselves to get lazy and just drift. They are disciplined—unbelievably disciplined.

Do you want to write a book, lose weight, or be successful with money? Get discipline.

Today's Winning Thought: Discipline is doing what you have to do even when you do not feel like it.

Drugs

medicinal substance; narcotic; hallucinogen

If you only pay attention to a few words in this book, be absolutely sure that you do not overlook this one. You need to have a healthy respect for drugs. They have a purpose. And casual use is not one of them. Be very serious about this. Too many lives have been ruined or ended because people made horrible decisions regarding the use of drugs. I chose to include this word in my top 100 after hearing yet another news report about a young person, a twenty-one-year-old man, who was found dead of a drug overdose. If you intentionally misuse or abuse drugs, you will find that it is a quick ticket to a miserable life, a life of pure hell. It could even be your death sentence.

And you can add alcohol to this.

Not long after I wrote about this word, a young promising major league baseball pitcher was killed in a boating accident. Jose Fernandez of the Miami Marlins was only twenty-four years old. A newspaper story stated that the autopsy report showed the player had cocaine and alcohol in his system. His blood-alcohol content level was 0.147, which is well above his state's legal limit of 0.08.

Today's Winning Thought: Please do not ignore the seriousness of this word.

Do-Over

second chance

If you are an athlete, you know that once the game begins there are no do-overs. Coaches can stop practice and rerun a play, but they do not have that luxury in a live game situation. Your do-over will have to come in the form of the next game or the next season.

Thankfully, life is not like that. You will more than likely get a do-over, a second chance. Do not take that for granted. Accept it for what it is—an opportunity to do things better, to do things right.

Zach Mettenberger is one young man who was given another chance. And he made good on it. Mettenberger was a highly recruited quarterback out of high school. He violated team rules and was dismissed from the University of Georgia Bulldogs before he could play a single down.

Mettenberger's second chance came a few weeks later when he enrolled at a community college. He had a good seasons there, on and off the field, and found a new home the following season at LSU. After three seasons at LSU, he was drafted by the NFL's Tennessee Titans.

Today's Winning Thought: If you run into trouble in life, you will most likely be granted a second chance. You might not be given a third or fourth chance. Make good on your do-over if you find yourself in that situation.

Dictionary

book explaining the meanings of alphabetically listed words, etc.

Every year, the Rotary Club I am a member of provides dictionaries to every third-grade student in our community. When we go, we share with them who we are and what Rotary does. We affix a bookplate inside the front cover. There, they can write their name. At the bottom of the sticker is also something known as The Four-Way Test. It is what Rotarians believe and strive to live by. (I share The Four-Way Test later in this book.)

The words you use, both written and spoken, mean a lot. It is important to be well-spoken. I told the students that their dictionary would be one of their best friends, if they learn to use it. I wish I would have realized that when I was younger. It took me nearly failing to graduate from high school to discover the importance of words, their definitions, and speaking with good diction. It served me well after I left high school, first as a radio broadcaster and later in my sales career.

Today's Winning Thought: Install a dictionary app on your phone and tablet and use it.

Doubters

be unsure or skeptical of; uncertainty or distrust;
something unsettled or uncertain

A friend of mine has some great children. Two of them are still in high school and play in the band. She told me one day that both of the girls occupy first chair. By definition, first chair is reserved for "the premier musician playing a particular instrument in an orchestra. That person is seated closest to the audience, taking the lead for that instrument's movements, and playing any solos."

The youngest girl is a freshman. She plays the saxophone. As I understand it, one day, a junior girl told her not to even bother with trying to earn first chair because freshmen never get to sit in first chair. Guess who is currently sitting in first chair? It is not the junior girl. It is my freshman friend.

Freshmen can earn first chair, if they have the talent and outwork everyone else.

You will always have doubters. And there will always be enough obstacles in your life. Do not add even more obstacles by believing the doubters. Believe in yourself and surround yourself with positive role models.

And don't you be a doubter. I was a doubter for a long time. I got into my own mind. I listened to my own negative self-talk, and I allowed it to discourage me. I wanted to write a book, but I did not believe I could. When I decided to try, I did not have the courage. When I found the courage, I did not have the discipline. Finally, I told myself I was going to complete my book. And I did. This is my second book. I also wanted to write a daily blog. I had no idea how to do that or where to start. I sought counsel and started writing *With Regard to Life* in 2009.

Listen to those who can help you, encourage you, and make you better.

Today's Winning Thought: Give no ear to those who doubt you.

Encouragement

give courage or resolution to

You will not need this word unless you are breathing. Push through the frustration, pain, and obstacles between you and the finish line. But if you are breathing, let me encourage you to live strong. Live the words in this book every day.

In his book, *It's Not Who You Know, It's Who You Are*, Pat Williams wrote about Green Bay Packers legend Bart Starr. Williams recalled a speech he had delivered at a waste management convention. He shared a message about empowering and encouraging people. Afterward, a man approached Williams and shared this story about Starr.

The man had started on the tail end of the garbage truck. Starr lived in one of the homes on his route. Often, the legendary quarterback would be outside and speak to the young man, ask how he was, and give him a word of encouragement. That motivated the young man, who had advanced to a management position in the company. He said, "The impact of Bart Starr on my life will never leave me."

Today's Winning Thought: Words spoken or written by you can have a powerful influence on another human. Make sure every word you say uplifts and inspires someone.

Execute

perform

An unnamed CEO once said that most companies that go out of business do not fail for lack of talent or strategic vision. They fail for lack of execution of the most basic things.

German novelist Johann Goethe said, "Knowing is not enough; we must apply. Willing is not enough; we must do."

Henry Ford, the American industrialist and inventor, added, "You cannot build a reputation on what you are going to do."

Before you can execute your plan, you have to begin. And sometimes, the hardest part of succeeding and getting to the next level is starting. It is often a matter of finding the energy and the drive to follow through and finish. Then, once you start, you have to do a little more, and work a little harder than others.

Today's Winning Thought: If your plans are not working, change them. If they are right, implement them.

Efficient / Effective

capable of producing desired results without wasting materials,
time and energy / producing desired result that is wanted

What do those words mean to you?

If you are efficient, you will produce the desired results without waste.

If you are effective, you will get the results you desire.

Author and speaker Les Parrott said effectiveness is a habit. He said it is built on practices.

Think of mechanics during a pit stop at the Indy 500. They make their decisions beforehand and then practice their drills. A wasted second by a member of the pit crew could be the difference in winning and losing and could cost a racing team millions of dollars.

In his book, *212: The Extra Degree*, S. L. Parker noted the average prize money for The Indianapolis 500 from 1993 to 2002. Parker wrote that the margin of victory was only 3.713 seconds. First place money was $1,378,771, while the average winnings for second place was $565,003. What was the difference in additional prize money for those three short seconds? 144 percent. Stated another way, it amounted to $813,768 *more* for the winner.

"If the ax is dull and its edge unsharpened, more strength is needed, but skill will bring success" (Ecclesiastes 10:10).

Abraham Lincoln also said as much when he stated, "Give me six hours to chop down a tree and I will spend the first four sharpening the axe."

Today's Winning Thought: Learn a skill. Stay sharp. Strive to be efficient and effective.

Effort

expenditure of strength, thought, etc.; attempt

Here is a way to all but ensure that you will not be very successful in life: just give little or no effort. Just do enough to get by. I am living proof. That was my mentality. I did just barely enough to get from one day to the next. And I was not living an abundant life. I was going nowhere fast.

My life did not change for the better until I changed. It took failing and a firing to get my attention. After I picked myself up and began to put forth even a small amount of effort, my life improved.

Today's Winning Thought: Learn every day, have a positive attitude, and give more than minimal effort. Do more than is expected of you, and do it without being asked.

Excellence

among the finest of its kind

Nothing or no one is perfect. But you can still strive for excellence.

Ralph Marston, a Texas businessman and writer of *The Daily Motivator*, once said, "Excellence is not a skill, it is an attitude." I agree with him. Here is a short story from MotivatesUs.com to support that idea.

A man stopped at a temple that was being built. He saw a sculptor making an idol of God. He noticed another similar idol on the ground. He inquired as to why the sculptor needed two idols. The sculptor told the onlooker that he only needed one, and that the one on the ground was damaged. The man could not see any noticeable damage. He asked where the damage was. The sculptor replied, "There is a scratch on the nose of the idol."

More discussion followed, and the visitor asked the sculptor where it was to be installed. He was told it was going to be placed on a pillar twenty feet above the ground. The man asked the sculptor who would possibly notice the scratch if it is twenty feet in the air. That question caused the sculptor to stop working. He looked at the man on the ground and replied, "I know it and God knows it."

That is an attitude of excellence rarely seen today.

Today's Winning Thought: *"The desire to excel should be exclusive of the fact whether someone appreciates it or not. Excellence is a drive from inside, not outside. Excel at a task today—not necessarily for someone else to notice but for your own satisfaction." (Author Unknown)*

Excuses

*attempt to lessen the blame attaching to a fault
or offense; seek to defend or justify*

I do not know who said this first, but I do know it is true. "If you're looking for an excuse, you'll always find one."

I could list a quote per day for the next year about making excuses. Allow me to include a couple of quotes about not making them. These are from successful athletes, who have had multiple opportunities to make an excuse if they wanted to. File these in the back of your mind. Carry them with you and memorize them.

"When I was younger, I was always taught not to make excuses." *(Derek Jeter, retired New York Yankees shortstop)*

"I HATE excuses. Excuses are a disease." (Cam Newton, NFL quarterback)

People do not want to hear excuses. They want to see results. They want to employ, work beside, and go through life with people who take responsibility for their lives. Do not tell me why you cannot do something. Instead, show me how you can.

Today's Winning Thought: You can get from failure to success, but not from excuses to success.

Faith

belief; confidence

My faith is an important part of my life. I will mention it a few times in this book. You might be a person of faith or you might not. Regardless of your beliefs, I am certain you will be encouraged by the words on these pages.

Here is a thought about faith. I like how author and pastor Max Lucado said it: "Faith is trusting what the eye can't see."

For me, that included trusting that God would give me the strength and courage to be a good husband and a good dad to a daughter who was born with Down syndrome. There was a time in my life, not too long before she was born, when I would have told you I could not deal with having a child with a developmental disability. Parenting was going to be a big enough change. Adding a child with mental retardation and a heart defect would probably be more than I could deal with.

I have learned that you can do more than you think you can when you have to. I found the strength I needed in my faith. I just had to remember that I could not do it in my own strength. Faith is all I had when a team of doctors told our family that there was nothing else they could do to save my daughter's life after she developed a virus following heart surgery.

John W. Barfield is one of America's greatest entrepreneurs. Barfield's granddaughter, Janan McDougall, is following his footsteps and becoming a strong businesswoman. She said about her grandfather, "He is a man who puts God first, his wife and family next, knowing that as long as he is doing right by them, everything else will naturally fall into place."

Today's Winning Thought: *"Many things in life will be beyond your control, so it is a good idea to get used to it and start developing your faith." (Dan Britton and Jimmy Page)*

Failure

attempt without success; not to do; disappoint; have no success; die away

Success begins with failure. Eric Weihenmayer has climbed the seven summits—the highest mountains on each continent, including Mt. Everest. Oh, and he is blind.

Weihenmayer has known success and failure. He said, "Success is not just the crowning moment, the spiking of the ball in the end zone, or the raising of the flag on the summit. It is the whole process of reaching for a goal, and sometimes it begins with failure."

I remember asking a friend a few weeks before my daughter was born if he would share with me the most important thing I should know about being a father for the first time. He immediately told me, with no hesitation, "Don't be afraid to let them fail."

Do not be afraid to fail. Do not be afraid to let your children fail. Learn from failure. Let it *refine* you and not *define* you.

Today's Winning Thought: *"Don't waste a failure by failing to learn from it." (Max Lucado)*

Fair

honest; just

If no one has ever told you this, let me be the first. Life is not always fair. Sometime in your life, you will be treated unfairly, be passed over for a job, or have something happen that might even cost you money. Don't fret over small stuff. Get over it and get on with your life. And take the high road when you do it.

In his book, *Mentor: The Kid and the CEO*, Tom Pace writes about a young man who had recently opened his own small business. One day, the young man told his mentor that an employee had quit to start his own similar business, and he was taking two other employees with him. On top of all of that, the employee had already secured his first job with a client of his former company. He got the bid by undercutting his former boss's bid.

Life was not fair to the young businessman in this case. We can all learn from what his mentor told him. The mentor told the young man to help his former employee. That is what he did. He called a company who chose the former employee to do some work and said they made a good choice and that they would be well taken care of.

It proved to be the right thing to do. The former employee later referred work back to this young businessman.

There might be times when the level of unfairness crosses the line. You should know your legal options and not be afraid to use them, when necessary. Most other times, control what you can and work through it.

Today's Winning Thought: Life is not always fair.

Family

group of relatives; group of related things

Family is very important. The breakdown of the traditional family is perhaps one of the greatest tragedies in America. Take care of your family. Make them a priority, not with your words, but with your actions.

I know a woman who has virtually no family to turn to. Her parents are deceased. Her relationship with her siblings is distant. Her marriages have ended. She is in financial ruin with nowhere to turn. She has burned more than one bridge. That is no way to live your life.

As I write this, I learned that she recently sought professional help. She has finally reached the point of no return and is trying to get her life on stable ground. If your life is in shambles, seek help before it is too late.

Your home should be a safe haven, a place you can go where you will be loved and supported. Families will experience trials and struggles and pain. You cannot avoid that. But your family should be your primary support system.

Today's Winning Thought: *"The love of family and the admiration of friends is much more important than wealth and privilege."* (Charles Kuralt)

Finish

to compete or bring to an end; to use up completely;
to perfect or complete by doing all things requisite
or desirable; to reach or come to an end

Later in this book, you will find the word *start*. This word is key—
finish what you start. Do not leave things undone. And don't just
finish, finish well. If you are flying, it is important to have a good
take off, but it is vital to have a good finish.

In sports and in life, it does not matter how you start. What matters most is how you finish. And do not quit too soon. Sometimes,
the game is won very late in the game, even on the final play.

Today's Winning Thought: Six-time NASCAR Champion
Jimmie Johnson said, "In order to finish first, first you must finish."

Friends

one who is well known by oneself and for whom
one has a warm regard or affection

If you do not have a friend you can call at 3 a.m. if you need to, you do not have deep enough friendships.

I use to carry a small square tile in my pocket to remind me of what it means to have true friends. The tile reminded me of a story in the gospel of Mark (Mark 2:1–5).

Jesus had returned home to Capernaum. The people had heard he was home. There were so many people that not everyone could even get near the home, much less enter it. Here (verse 3) is where the friends come in.

"Some men came, bringing to him a paralytic, carried by four of them. The men could not get their friend to Jesus because of the large crowd. So, they made an opening in the roof and lowered the mat the paralyzed man was lying on."

The needs of this paralytic moved his friends to action, and they brought him to Jesus.

Today's Winning Thought: Do you respond like these men did when you see people, particularly your friends, who have a need?

Forgiveness

regard without ill will despite an offense

It will not always be easy, but you will be much happier and a lot stronger if you learn to forgive.

Do not carry a grudge. A grudge can get pretty heavy. Do not carry a scorecard. Being an unforgiving person can poison you. Life can be difficult enough. Do not make it worse by refusing to forgive. You, and others around you, will be miserable. And the individual you need to forgive will likely live happily ever after.

Today's Winning Thought: *"When you forgive, you in no way change the past, but you sure do change the future." (Bernard Meltzer)*

Goals

object to be reached or attained

Burn Your Goals!

That is the title of a book I read. It was written by Joshua Medcalf and Jamie Gilbert. When I saw the title, I knew I had to read it. I was a bit uncertain, but I am a believer now. You will be too, if you read it. I encourage you to do so.

Here are a few things the men wrote.

"I didn't have GOALS. All I tried to do was love people, serve people, provide value, and God took me places beyond my wildest dreams."

"Burn your wish list. I want to know that you have a commitment list. I want to know what you are committed to doing with your 24 hours a day to close the gap between where you are and where you want to be. What are you willing to sacrifice inside your 86,400 seconds every day to become the person you want to be?"

"Rather than focusing on arbitrary goals, we try to focus 100 percent of our energy on our commitments and controlables."

They added that if you focus on goals, you increase pressure and decrease confidence, and that will make you miserable. As I thought about that, I realized that they are exactly right.

Today's Winning Thought: *"Stop setting goals. Goals are pure fantasy unless you have a plan to achieve them." (Stephen Covey)*

Grace

kindness or favor

Real grace, free and unmerited, is powerful. It is life-giving. A pastor and friend said grace frees us and opens life, and it enriches our lives and others as we give grace.

Our daughter participates in Special Olympics. One of the sports she is involved in is basketball. If you have ever watched one of these games, you will soon notice almost immediately that there is more than a fair amount of grace given in the way the contests are officiated. The first double dribble or traveling violation will normally occur within the first five seconds of the game. But you will never see it called. That is just the way it is in this game.

I have received much grace for the mistakes in my life, which are far more serious than any basketball infraction. I am thankful for that. I am also trying to be mindful about extending grace to others.

Today's Winning Thought: Learn that one well. You will have countless opportunities in this life.

Grow

become; develop; cause to live

I do not make New Year's resolutions. More than 85 percent of people who make resolutions fail to keep them beyond a few days. Instead of one or more resolution, I focus on something I learned from Dan Britton, Jimmy Page, and Jon Gordon, who authored *One Word*. The premise is you can focus on a single word and create clarity that will bring about life change.

A few years ago, my word for the year was *grow*. I wanted to . . .

Grow in my knowledge of God.

Replenish more often.

Get and stay *organized*.

Write with purpose.

The next year, my one word was *today*. Yesterday is gone. There is no chance of getting that time back. Tomorrow is not here, and there is no guarantee that I will live to see it. All I have is today. What I do today will affect every tomorrow that I am given.

Even though my one word changes at the beginning of every year, growing is something I continually strive for. I did not want to stop growing in my knowledge of God at the end of that year. I still want to replenish more often, get and stay organized, and write with purpose. And I want those things every year for the rest of my life.

Today's Winning Thought: Personal growth is worth the investment.

Hope

to desire with expectations fulfillment

You can live about six weeks without food. You can live about six minutes without air. You can live about three days without water.

What about hope? How long can you live without hope? Don't take any chances. I would treat hope like it was air.

People need hope. Hope is a powerful force. Determination can help provide that hope.

The late Zig Ziglar once said that there are seldom any hopeless situations, only people who have lost hope. Stay strong, even when your situation looks bleak. *Never* lose hope.

Today's Winning Thought: *"What oxygen is to the lungs, hope is to the meaning of life." (Anonymous)*

Hustle

move or act energetically

The following sentence is the first sentence in Joshua Medcalf's book *Hustle*.

"Hustle is the most important word ever." That is a quote from Gary Vaynerchuk.

Medcalf wrote that dreams are free but hustle is sold separately.

Hustle is a good word, an important word, but I would question if it is the most important word ever. You need to hustle, but don't hurry. You need to work smart, work hard, seize opportunities, adapt to change, always be learning and growing, and always striving to be better.

The title of the last chapter in the book I just mentioned is "Don't Die with It Trapped Inside." "It" is your potential. Don't die with your potential, your dreams, and your greatness trapped inside you.

Today's Winning Thought: Go all out in this life. To do that, you will have to hustle.

History

account of the past; known or recorded past

One of my regrets is that I did not pay close enough attention in school, particularly in history class. That was the hour I chose to go sit with a few buddies at a fast-food hamburger place.

I was so immature, so careless with what clearly should have mattered to me—my education.

I wish I would have attended class more and paid attention. I would be wiser than I am today.

History should have been important to me, and it should be important to you, because . . .

It can inspire you.

It teaches you more about the world and how we got to this point.

It will help you understand the world better.

It can make you a better citizen.

If you are still in school, go to class, pay attention, and learn something. If you are out of school, you can still learn. That is when my real learning started.

Today's Winning Thought: *"The student who learns history will unconsciously develop what is the highest value of history: judgment in worldly affairs. We gather historical knowledge, not to make us more clever the next time, but wiser for all time." (Jacques Barzun (adapted))*

Intentional

As I have mentioned in this book, I do not make New Year's resolutions. Instead, I try to live by one specific word each year. One of the words I have tried to live by in the word *intentional*. Here is what being intentional looks like for me.

Invest.

Now.

Today.

Expect success.

New.

Think every day.

Inspire people.

Organize.

Nurture relationships.

Adapt, adopt, or abandon.

Live urgently.

Someone once said that the difference between ordinary and extraordinary is a little extra.

What would it take for you to be a little better tomorrow than you are today? What would it take for you to be a little better off financially and physically tomorrow than you are today? A little extra effort. You can only get that little extra by being intentional.

Today's Winning Thought: What do you want your life to look like five years from today? Ten years? The road to your future starts right where you are—today! Have a plan. Be intentional about living it and making adjustments, when needed.

Illiteracy

unable to read

Today, too many youngsters are living in a prison without walls. Many of them do not even know it. That prison is illiteracy.

Thomas Bloch, former chairman of the board of H & R Block, wrote in his book *Stand for the Best*, "Socioeconomic factors, including parental involvement and home life, are critical influences in a child's academic performance. Literacy is a bridge from misery to hope. It is a tool for daily life in a modern society. It is a bulwark against poverty."

Literacy and education is the roadmap to hope and success. Sadly, many do not know it. They are stuck in a cycle.

World Vision president Richard Sterns said, "No long-term escape from poverty is possible without the methodical and routine education of children—both boys and girls."

If you are in school, take advantage of the wonderful opportunity you have. I did not, and it nearly cost me. Do not take your education for granted. And do not stop learning when you leave high school or college. That is when real learning begins.

Today's Winning Thought: Breaking the cycle of poverty is a war we must win. Literacy is one of our major weapons.

Integrity

firmness of character; honesty

If you lose this, you lose.

Someone was once asked to define business ethics. The answer was there is no such thing as business ethics. There is only ethics. You either have them all the time or you don't.

Maintain your integrity, starting with the little things. If you do, you will be able to be trusted with even bigger things. I will never be able to say it any better than W. Clement Stone, who said, "Have the courage to say no. Have the courage to face the truth. Do the right thing because it is right. These are the magic keys to living your life with integrity."

Or as R. E. Littlejohn noted, "Guard your integrity. There is no excuse for even a little dishonesty. It takes years to build trust and only seconds to destroy it. Wear your moral compass like a wristwatch, and consult it regularly."

Today's Winning Thought: *"Do the right thing, and get caught doing it." (John Diamond)*

Joy

intense happiness; joy of this

I am a happy guy. Not only am I happy, I am blessed. I am joyful.

That is what you would really rather be—joyous rather than happy. Do not confuse the two. Our joy should not fluctuate or be dependent upon our circumstances. Every day, we must choose to make a conscious decision to be joyful. Happiness will come and go. Joy will get you through the storms of life.

Be joyful always, especially when you face trials. That is what the scriptures tell us to do (James 1:2–3). "Consider it pure joy, my brothers, whenever you face trials of many kinds, because you know that the testing of your faith develops perseverance."

Today's Winning Thought: Joy defeats discouragement; happiness just covers it up.

Kindness

benevolence; compassionate

A little kindness will go a long way. Always remember that. It is what you would want.

What is kindness? It is being considerate, gentle, generous, tolerant, unselfish, compassionate, helpful, and cordial. It means that we should serve, listen, and show respect for fellow human beings. We can all do that. Being kind does not require a lot of time, and it does not have to cost money. You just have to be intentional.

A sixth grader summed it up pretty well when he said, "If someone is in need, just lend a hand and help them out."

If it is that simple why don't more people show kindness?

Today's Winning Thought: *"Common courtesy benefits everyone and enriches our personal and professional lives. The Golden Rule—treat others like you want to be treated—is the best human relations rule known to man." (Zig Ziglar)*

Live

be alive; dwell; spend one's life; depend for existence; experience or spend; alive; vital; electrically charged

Before I talk about this word, let me say that I do not like the word *dwell*, at least for this definition. *Dwell* means having one's habitation, or lingering, as in speech or thought. Far be it for me to add or remove anything from the dictionary, so I will leave it. Just know that I want you to do more than just exist. I want you to not just have a place to live. I want you to really live. I hope you love life and that you will live your life to the fullest. I hope you will be truly blessed.

Know this: Life is short regardless of the number of years we live. So be intentional. Do not waste heartbeats. Do not take life—yours or the people who mean the most to you—for granted. Because too soon, it will be gone.

I wrote this part of the book less than an hour after visiting a close friend, a gentleman who was a mentor to me. I learned only a few hours earlier that he had been diagnosed with cancer. Two weeks prior to that, I was standing at the bedside of another great friend, who was also battling cancer.

Life can turn on a dime. Live fully. Live intentionally. Live expectantly. Live to serve. Live to give. Live today. That is all you have. Learn from yesterday. Plan for tomorrow and for the future. But today is all we really have. We are guaranteed nothing more.

I once read that we will all leave a legacy. We are writing it every day. Take care of the minutes. They will add up to hours, the hours will turn into days, and the days will become weeks, and months, and years.

Today's Winning Thought: Today, live your life to the fullest and with no regrets.

Lessons

something learned at one time

I have listed sixty-one lessons here. Why sixty-one? That was my age when I began writing the book. I wish I would have learned these life lessons earlier in my life while I was in middle school or high school. I eventually learned them, many of them the hard way. I believe they are so critical to success in life that I have included them in this book.

First, let me ask you a question which I read on Twitter recently. What will you do today to make tomorrow the best day ever? Learning these lessons will help you have a brighter tomorrow.

Some of these are mentioned in other parts of this book. In no particular order, here is my list:

Have a positive attitude. Remember the first word in this book? If something, a job, for instance, comes down to two people—you and one other—the person with the best attitude will get the job most of the time.

Do not be arrogant. People hate arrogance.

Be gracious and humble.

Be teachable and coachable.

Think big.

Think within reach.

Take affordable next steps.

Don't complain. If you do, you need to have a workable solution which allows everyone to win.

No excuses. People hate excuses just like they hate arrogance. Maybe even more.

Do not take shortcuts. They end up being more costly.

Overcome your past. Dr. Henry Cloud said, "At some point, 'That is how he was raised' ceases to be an excuse."

Get wisdom, even if it costs you everything you have.

Life is not always fair.

Life is not about you.

Do not be afraid to fail. Jeff Goins said, "Failure is not what prevents us from success. It is what leads us there."

"Never allow a mistake to become another one," said former National Football League referee Red Cashion.

Do not quit too soon.

Read! Read! Read!

Learn about personal accountability and live that way.

Stop every day and just think.

Learn how to communicate with people. You will need to know this.

Listen well.

Write well.

Spell correctly.

Understand money and learn how to manage what you have.

Eliminate and avoid debt.

Volunteer.

Do not assume anything—ever.

Do not take people or things for granted—ever.

Have all the facts you need to make decisions.

Tell the truth.

Trust your instincts

Help a child learn to read.

Protect children.

Protect and invest in your relationships.

Encourage people.

Do not become a victim. Help others avoid having a victim mentality.

Be forgiving.

Never lose hope.

Be very responsible with all drugs.

Take care of the minutes. They become hours, then days, then weeks.

Find work you enjoy. Know your purpose, and why you do what you do.

Appreciate the arts.

Have a sense of humor.

Have a vision for your life.

Have a plan for your life.

Be relentless. Basketball analyst Jay Bilas said it is hard to beat relentless.

Ask for advice from people you trust. Follow it.

Get an accountability partner.

Differentiate yourself.

Dress nicely.

Buy quality products.

Do not expect anything to be handed to you.

Do more than is expected of you.

Expect the unexpected.

Give yourself a chance.

Give yourself some margin.

Work smart.

Work hard.

Don't hold grudges.

Look both ways twice before pulling away from an intersection.

Today's Winning Thought: There are countless other life lessons. Learn as many of them as you can, and learn them early in life.

Learn

come to know; know how

I received the shock of my life late in my senior year of high school. I knew I had not been paying attention like I should have been. I skipped a lot of classes. I wasted that time at a local fast-food hangout when I should have been studying. Simply put, I really could have cared less about school. Then, reality hit me like a truck. I flunked a class. I did not meet the number of class credits required to graduate. As it turned out, I had an extra credit in physical education and I was able to graduate.

It was that day that I started learning—about life. School was now in session. I could change my attitude and succeed, or I could remain lethargic and continue down a road that would lead me to places I did not want to go.

You have probably heard the phrase, "Sometimes you win, sometimes you lose." John Maxwell said it better in his book, *Sometimes You Win, Sometimes You Learn.* Maxwell wrote, "Losing gives us an opportunity to learn, but many people do not seize it. And when they don't, losing really hurts." I was losing at life, but I took advantage of the opportunity to learn. You have to want to learn. You will never regret learning from your mistakes and setbacks.

Today's Winning Thought: Knowledge is power. But it is really more than that. Amy Gutmann, president of the University of Pennsylvania, said, "Knowledge is not only power, but also a catalyst for progress."

Lose

fail to keep; misplace; fail to win

I heard a college baseball coach say one day that he wanted his team to refuse to lose.

That is a good mind-set. I do not believe you should enjoy losing, nor expect to lose. But the reality is you will lose from time to time. You cannot win every time. When that happens, adopt the mind-set of another coach I know. My friend retired as one of the winningest coaches in junior college football. During his final season, his team lost three games. All were close and came down to the final seconds. After one of the losses, he tweeted, "We lost a game, not a season."

We can apply that to our own lives. A loss will not ruin you, nor define you, but it can strengthen you. Pick yourself up off the ground, brush yourself off and get going again.

Today's Winning Thought: Businessman and author Harvey Mackay wrote, "It doesn't matter how much milk you spill, just don't lose the cow."

Little

small; petty; not much; short while; small amount

My pastor said once that it is not the tire that has the blowout that gets you, it is the one with a slow leak. You notice the blowout. It gets your attention immediately. The slow leak is gradual. You are moving along and things begin to change, slowly, little by little, then noticeably.

Watch those little things in life. If you don't, one day, you will be some place you do not want to be, and you will wonder how you ended up there. You might end up like the ship that was only a degree off course, but that was enough to make it veer hundreds of miles from its planned destination.

It works the other way too. Greatness begins with doing something, a little thing, very well. Former college basketball coach George Raveling said, "All great things begin as a small thing."

Do not overlook the little things.

Today's Winning Thought: *"It is the little details that are vital. Little things make big things happen."* (John Wooden)

Loyalty

faithful

I asked a few people while I was writing this book to share with me one word that they believed was critical to a person's success in life. Two of them, my dentist and a friend who is a coach and athletic director, both shared this word. Without any hesitation, both of them said *loyalty* is the word they would suggest.

Loyalty is a faithfulness or devotion to an oath or obligation, and it comes, over time, from dedication.

My friend's son is a Marine. She shared an article with me about leadership traits of Marines. These traits, fourteen of them, are the basic fundamentals that Marines use to develop their own leadership abilities and that of their subordinates. One of the traits is loyalty, which the Marines define in this way:

Loyalty: The quality of faithfulness to country, the Corps, and unit, and to one's seniors, subordinates, and peers. The motto of our Corps is *Semper Fidelis,* Always Faithful. You owe unswerving loyalty and down the chain of command: to seniors, subordinates, and peers.

Jeffrey Gitomer, a well-known sales trainer, said, "You don't learn loyalty in a day. You learn it day by day."

Be loyal to your team, to your employer and stakeholders, and to your family. Have their backs in good times and in the battles.

Today's Winning Thought: *"Where the battle rages, the loyalty of the soldier is proved." (Martin Luther)*

Margin

border or border area; difference in amounts

The sooner you learn the true meaning of this word, the better off you are going to be. Learn now to spend less than you make, to have a savings or a reserve. I am talking specifically about money, but it also goes for other resources. And learn to allow yourself margin of time.

Today's Winning Thought: You will never regret having a little extra money, time, and resources than you need. You will be stressed out and maybe even overwhelmed if you don't.

Mentor

teacher or advisor

Every Monday morning for several years, I met my friend, George, for breakfast. He was more than a friend. He was a mentor. He was quiet, caring, and very wise about business and life. When George talked, I listened because I knew he would have something important to say. I learned a lot by watching him and listening to him. He was one who I wanted serving with me on any committee I chaired. It simply made me and the committee better.

It is wise to have a mentor. Most successful people do. I would encourage you to find someone who can coach you and help you be more successful.

Veteran athletes often have their cubicle in the corner of the locker room near several younger players. There is a lot of teaching that goes on there during the course of the season. The older veteran players teaching the younger players how they can be better players and teammates.

Today's Winning Thought: Finding a mentor will be one of the best decisions and investments you will ever make.

Mistakes

wrong act or opinion

You are going to make mistakes in your life. Remember this about mistakes:

Make them early in life. Learn while you are young.

Own them.

Fix them.

Do not repeat them.

Do not make careless stupid mistakes.

Learn from your mistakes.

In most instances, making a mistake is just a bend in the road. Former National Football League referee Red Cashion once said, "A bend in the road is not the end of the road, unless you fail to make the turn."

You risk failing to negotiate the turns in life when you have a poor attitude, you are not willing to learn, when you do not give your best effort and when you are obstinate.

A mistake is an opportunity to begin again. Make your mistakes work for you, not against you.

Today's Winning Thought: *"Don't let what is behind you define you or it will confine you." (James Ford Jr.)*

Money

paper or metal accepted everywhere in payment of debts

If you truly want to enjoy your life, there are a few things you have to get right. This one is critical. You must have a thorough understanding of money. If you cannot read and do not manage your money well, you will likely have a long and unhappy life.

Money will either bring you peace or the lack of it will bring you misery. I have experienced both. I have been blessed and I have been miserable. I was the most miserable when I was irresponsible and stupid with money. Please do not be either of those. Peace is better, I promise.

Remembering these things will put you in a position to win with money.

Live within your means. Spend less than you make.

Get out of debt as quickly as you can. And stay out.

Today's Winning Thought: Save some money every month. Even a small amount, saved consistently when you are young, can make you wealthy.

Never

not ever; not at any time

Never cosign a loan for someone.

Never, never, never get an advance at a payday loan business. Never!

Medical debt is one of the leading causes of bankruptcy. Understand the need for and purchase adequate insurance.

Do not put all of your financial eggs in one basket.

If you are in middle or high school and are planning to go to college, you will want to read this closely. Then, read it again.

In 2015, financial expert Dave Ramsey and his daughter, Rachel Cruse, wrote an article titled "3 Shocking Facts Every Parent Needs to Know." These numbers are shocking. If you put yourself in a similar situation, your life will be miserable.

The article noted that 60 percent of college freshmen max out a credit card the first year.

It also stated that the class of 2013 graduates averaged $35,200 in total debt.

And finally, 59 percent of kids, according to the article, feel they could be smarter about money.

Being poor is expensive. The poor will generally pay more for cars and insurance. They will pay higher interest rates. They are unable to buy in bulk or receive discounts for paying with cash. The poor will rely on debt. They will buy processed foods rather than food that will give them better health. You have fewer options when you are poor.

Today's Winning Thought: Do not be like those young people. Get some knowledge about money and a little self-discipline to go with it. I promise you will not regret it.

Opportunities

favorable occasion

I read an article once titled "Great Opportunities, Great Opposition." You need to look for opportunities, evaluate them, and take advantage of the good ones. Be sure that you have enough margin in your life. Without margin, you might not be able to pursue many opportunities when they present themselves.

You rarely have to look for opposition. Opposition will find you. It can also be good for you. Embrace opposition. The right amount of tension can strengthen us, and make us better.

It might help you to look at opposition as opportunities, which they generally are. A problem is defined as a situation involving difficulty. An opportunity is a favorable juncture of circumstance.

Do not give up and quit too soon. Opportunities are often disguised as opposition.

Today's Winning Thought: *"Failure is the opportunity to begin again, more intelligently." (Henry Ford)*

Overcome

get the better of

Liz Murray survived a horrible childhood. As a teenager, she was homeless. She overcame those extreme challenges and attended Harvard, where she earned her degree.

Ms. Murray and her sister grew up with parents who were drug addicts. She said even though her parents were shooting up every day, and every minute of every day was utter chaos, the girls felt loved by their parents.

Ms. Murray's mother died of AIDS. Eventually, she found herself living on the streets of Manhattan. She worked in a supermarket when she was nine so she could eat. The young woman grew up fast, she had no choice. She realized one day that she was repeating her mother's life. Except Liz was not on drugs. She wrote, "I had to keep going, even when I was in this situation."

One day in the midst of the ongoing turmoil, Ms. Murray said, "No one owes me anything. I will make it through this on my own. I had the idea that I could be responsible for my own life."

It is almost certain that you have had a better start in life than Liz Murray did. It is very important that you learn the life lessons she learned.

She had to be responsible.

No one owed her anything.

She had to keep on going.

Things can happen.

Do not put limits on yourself.

Today's Winning Thought: Liz Murray's story can make us look at life differently.

Partner

*one who is united or associated with another
or others in some action or enterprise*

I was visiting with a Starbucks manager one day, and we were discussing the way her team was working so well together. They all seemed to get along, and the place was running very smoothly, as expected. It was clear they loved their jobs and they loved their customers. That happens, I believe, because they all view each other as partners. It even says as much on the back of their business cards.

We're looking for more than employees; we are looking for partners. That is what we call every single employee who works at Starbucks. And if you ask partners why they enjoy working here, they'll probably tell you it's the opportunity to make meaningful connections and have an impact every day by working some place truly great.

I was reading a trade magazine recently. There was a quote that drives home the importance of partnerships. It was from Steve Slagle, who was being inducted into the Promotional Products Association International Hall of Fame.

"Without a doubt I can say that almost everything I accomplished or was given credit for was done in partnership with volunteers and staff," Slagle said.

Today's Winning Thought: It is likely that you will be in a partnership someday. Maybe in business, maybe in sports or maybe in marriage. Be a good partner. And know that you will not accomplish everything by yourself.

Personal Accountability

answerable; responsible

Abraham Lincoln said, "You cannot escape the responsibility of tomorrow by evading it today."

John Miller wrote a book that I believe should be required reading for every middle and high school student before they can graduate. It is titled *QBQ: The Question behind the Question.*

QBQ is all about personal accountability. It is about eliminating blame, complaining, and procrastination.

The best two questions you can ask are *What can I do?* and *How can I help?* Get this book and read it. You can read it during lunch. Then, challenge your friends to read it.

One more thought on personal accountability. If you get this wrong, it could kill you.

Driving a car is a privilege, not a right. There are traffic laws for a reason, a good reason. They are there to make driving safer for everyone. You put your life and the lives of others in danger when you drive too fast and too carelessly. Put your phone down. Be a safe, courteous, and responsible driver.

Today's Winning Thought: Make personal accountability a core value in your life.

Purpose

intention; object

"This is your time, your moment. Don't miss it."

Those words rang in my ears for several days after I read them. I still cannot get them out of my mind, years after I first saw them. It is something novelist Stephen King told graduates during a commencement address a Vassar College. They are as relevant today as they were when he spoke them in 2001.

I believe each one of us has a purpose, something we are supposed to do. And there has never been a better time than today to start carrying out your purpose. We have a short window of opportunity to make a difference. Our time on this earth is limited. Start living today.

Today's Winning Thought: This is your time, your moment. Don't miss it.

Passion

strong feeling or emotion

How does a rock singer like Elton John or rock groups like The Beach Boys and The Rolling Stones keep performing six decades after they started?

One word: Passion. That is what Mick Jagger of The Rolling Stones said once when asked that question. It is a passion for what they do that has enabled these people to keep performing their music.

Passion is the key for many people. I read once that when he was a teenager, celebrity chef Bobby Flay was going nowhere fast. He was walking around aimlessly, until he discovered the world of cooking. Today, he is a household name with a small empire.

I am not saying that if you find a passion for something that you will automatically become rich or famous. What I will tell you is if you add determination to detail, a strong work ethic, an intense desire for quality and be good to the people on your team, you will succeed. It is up to you.

Today's Winning Thought: *"Most people don't lead their own lives—they accept their lives." (John Kotter)*

Quit

abandon

Ecclesiastes 3:6 says, "There is a time to search and a time to give up."

It is difficult for me to give up, lose hope, and quit. Part of the reason might be because of what we experienced with our daughter, Kyle. She was born with Down syndrome and a heart defect. She underwent life-saving surgery when she was seventeen months old. The surgery was successful, but she developed a virus while she was hospitalized. Her condition deteriorated to the point that her team of doctors said there was nothing more they could do to save her. Then, doctors changed some medicine and saved her life. We witnessed a miracle during those days, so forgive me if I have a thing about quitting easily or too soon.

Give careful consideration before you quit. You might be very close to succeeding.

Author and speaker Andy Andrews said, "You must know in the game of life, nothing is less important than the score at halftime. The tragedy of life is not that man loses, but that he almost wins."

There are other things in life that you should quit. You should quit them today—immediately!

Quit complaining.

Quit procrastinating.

Quit wasting your money and resources.

Quit wasting your time and your life on things that do not matter.

Quit obsessing over things you cannot change.

Quit doing things that are detrimental to your physical and mental health.

Quit doing things that are bad for your relationships.

Quit doing things that are keeping you from being your best.

Today's Winning Thought: Do not quit easy or without cause. But if you need to quit doing something that is potentially destructive, do it now and never look back.

Relationships

the fact or condition of being connected in some way

Life is all about relationships. Relationships with your parents, your siblings, your extended family, your friends, your teammates, your coworkers, your employer, and your customers. Do not take the people in your life for granted. Value your relationships. Invest in them. Nurture them.

I am in sales. I do not want one order from a customer. I want a relationship—a long-term relationship. I want friends and clients. In fact, as I consider my clients, many of them have done business with me for many years. They can purchase their products from countless other vendors. They work with my company because theirs is a trust, a relationship.

Relationships take effort. Over time, they grow stronger.

Today's Winning Thought: Be the person everybody wants to be around. The one everyone wants to seek out for advice.

Read

to look at and understand the meaning of letters, words, symbols, etc.

Read! Read! Read! It is one of the very best things you can do for yourself.

"Regular reading not only boosts the likelihood of an individual's academic and *economic success*—facts that are not especially surprising—but it also seems to awaken a person's social and civic sense." ("To Read or Not to Read," NEA 2007)

Charles Scribner II, a publisher in the mid-1800s, said, "Reading is a means of thinking with another person's mind. It forces you to stretch your own."

I was having lunch with a college reading instructor recently. I asked her if she could confirm a statistic I had heard—that nearly 60 percent of students entering college need some kind of remedial reading. She did not know the exact percentage, but she did agree it is a serious problem. At the time of our visit, she had one student—remember, this is college—who was reading at the first grade level. That is unacceptable and inexcusable in America today. There is a very real cost when individuals cannot read.

Here is a challenge for you. I want you to read a book every two weeks. If you cannot do that, read a book every month. Here are some suggested titles for getting started. These are in no particular order. Just grab and read as many of them as you can.

QBQ by John Miller
Flipping the Switch by John Miller
The Energy Bus by Jon Gordon
The Shark and the Goldfish by Jon Gordon
Do Over by Jon Acuff
START by Jon Acuff

The Sender by Kevin Elko and Bill Beauty

2 Chairs by Bob Beanie

The Hope Quotient by Ray Johnston

Chase the Lion by Mark Batterson

The Art of Work by Jeff Goins

The Power of Small by Linda Kaplan Thaler and Robin Koval

212: The Extra Degree by S. L. Parker

Starting from Scratch: The Humble Beginnings of a Two-Billion Dollar Enterprise by John W. Barfield

We Got Fired by Harvey Mackay

Pushing the Envelope by Harvey Mackay

3 Seconds by Les Parrott

Embrace the Struggle by Zig Ziglar

Better Than Good by Zig Ziglar

Failing Forward by John Maxwell

The Noticer by Andy Andrews

Mastering the Seven Decisions by Andy Andrews

Rhinoceros Success by Scott Alexander

The Janitor by Todd Hopkins and Ray Hilbert

Holy Discontent by Bill Hybels

Total Money Makeover by Dave Ramsey

The Pursuit by Pat Williams

Onward by Howard Schultz

The Secret Blend by Stan Toler

The Max Strategy by Dale Dauten

Simplify by Bill Hybels

Refuel by Doug Fields

The Positive Dog by Jon Gordon

The Seed by Jon Gordon

Training Camp by Jon Gordon

The Go Giver by Bob Burg and David Mann

The Present by Spencer Johnson

The Dip [or another title] by Seth Godin
Sometimes You Win, Sometimes You Learn by John Maxwell
If by Mark Patterson
All In by Mark Batterson
Burn Your Goals by Joshua Medcalf and Jamie Gilbert
Thinking for a Change by John Maxwell
Today Matters by John Maxwell
The 15 Laws of Growth by John Maxwell
The Carpenter by Jon Gordon
The Mentor and the CEO by Tom Pace
Up, Down, and Sideways by Mark Sanborn
The Fred Factor by Mark Sanborn
Swim with the Sharks without Being Eaten Alive by Harvey Mackay
It's Not Who You Know, It's Who You Are by Pat Williams
Upside Down by Marv Loucks
The Bible

Today's Winning Thought: *"Reading is your secret weapon to change both who you become and the overall trajectory of your life."* *(Joshua Medcalf, author of* Burn Your Goals)

Resilient

*springing back to a former shape or position; capable of recoiling
from pressure or shock unchanged or undamaged; elastic, buoyant*

I once watched a college football team win a game they had no business winning. They were behind by three touchdowns in the second half and were struggling to score and stop their opponent from scoring. They kept playing, one down at a time, one possession at a time. No excuses, no finger pointing, no blame game. Just focus and effort. This was a resilient bunch. They recoiled from pressure or shock unchanged and undamaged. And I believe, they are now better players and men because of it.

Life is like football. Sometime in your life, probably several times, you are going to face adversity. Be resilient. Stay positive. Don't point fingers, don't make excuses, and do not blame others. That will not lead you to a successful outcome. Stop, take a deep breath, and keep working through whatever you are facing. You will get through whatever you are dealing with and be a stronger person because of it.

Today's Winning Thought: *"Constant detours do not bring a man into the presence of greatness. Detours do not build muscle. Detours do not provide life's lessons. Between you and anything significant will be giants in your path." (Andy Andrews)*

Respect

esteem; honor; consideration; deference

Early in the first week of spring training prior to the start of the 2015 major league baseball season, Chicago Cubs manager Joe Maddon shared with his players what he called Respect 90. Maddon was emphasizing the importance of being fundamentally sound and respecting the game. Doing the right thing, the right way every time. Doing things like running hard to first base (90 feet) on a ground ball.

His philosophy worked. The Cubs went further in the playoffs than they had in many years, and Maddon was named National League Manager of the Year.

These were major league players, the best in the game, receiving reminders about something very important to their success. If it is good enough for a team of professionals, it is good enough for you and me. It is vital that we respect the game, if you will. Respect your work, respect your team, respect the process, respect yourself, and respect life. Respect the game. Not so you can be named Manager of the Year, but because it is the right thing to do.

Today's Winning Thought: We should all give and be given respect because we are God's creation. But real respect is earned, not given. You do not earn the respect of your peers and your leaders by being lazy, giving minimal effort and just getting by. That will not lead to respect or success.

Risk

chance of defeat, injury or loss

A ship is safe in the harbor, but that is not what ships were made for.

Likewise, we were not created to sit idly and coast through life. I have not found who to attribute this quote to, but you should let it guide you.

"To love is to risk rejection, to live is to risk dying, and to hope is to risk failure. But risk must be taken because the greatest hazard in life is to risk nothing at all."

I heard a *New York Times* bestselling author say that he failed once and that his boss was perfectly fine with it. He was okay with it because there are two kinds of failure. There is failure that comes from trying something new or better or additional to make something even better. Experimentation is necessary. And there is failure because of laziness and poor effort or no effort. That is not acceptable.

Do not risk your personal safety or your life or that of your family. Lives cannot be replaced. Count the cost. Do not risk everything you own. But there will certainly be times when taking a calculated risk is the right thing to do.

Today's Winning Thought: A calculated risk is one that has been subjected to calculation. It is something you arrived at after weighing all the circumstances.

Small

little; of no great importance, value, etc.; petty or
mean; into small pieces; narrow part

Emily Dickinson said you can gain more control over your life by playing closer attention to the little things.

Linda Kaplan Thaler and Robin Koval coauthored a book that speaks to that. It is titled *The Power of Small*. Here is a great story from their book.

It seems a major restaurant chain—a client of the authors—was losing a lot of money because crystal was breaking much too frequently. It reached the point that regional and district managers met to search for solutions to the problem. New training programs were discussed as was replacing the crystal with a different brand of glassware. A busboy overheard the executives' conversation and pulled one of them aside. They walked to the kitchen, which is where the problem was. The busboy showed the executive how the commercial dishwasher vibrated. Repeated vibration might have ultimately led to the breakage, the busboy thought. He was right. It was a small detail that saved the company millions of dollars over a period of years.

I do not know if the busboy received a promotion, but the story in the book stated that he did receive a bonus from the company—a $150,000 tip!

Today's Winning Thought: Do you think small details are not important? Think again.

Serve

act in the service of a person, organization or cause; be of use to

I was looking through one of my bookshelves recently for ideas to write about in my blog. My eyes stopped at one titled *Adventures in Service.* The book, which is about Rotary, was given to me by a friend. My friend was not a Rotarian, but his father was. He said he thought of me when he found the book and he wanted me to have it.

The message from the short book is that when one becomes a member of a Rotary Club, he or she begins an adventure in service. One of the primary goals of Rotary is to put into practice the philosophy of Service Above Self. That motto is based on the practical, ethical advice that he who profits most serves best.

One of the greatest things you can ever do is serve others. Be a servant. Put others before yourself. Do not cross the street to avoid someone who is in need of help, like the priest and Levite did in the parable of the Good Samaritan. Instead, do what the Samaritan did. Reach out and serve those with real needs. It will not always be pleasant or convenient, but more often than not you will be blessed.

Today's Winning Thought: Each one of us has a gift, and some have more than one. It is my belief that we are to use those gifts to serve others.

Start

begin; beginning

Sometimes, the hardest part of a task or project is getting started. That might be because you do not know where to start. Or you lack some key piece of information or material. Or maybe you are lazy or undisciplined. That used to be my problem.

One example was with money. I waited too many years to start living with a financial plan and saving money. If that is you, do not wait. Start saving some amount of money. Start today! You will likely live to regret it if you don't. My wife and I once worked with a financial planner who encouraged us to start an Individual Retirement Account. He walked us through what the IRA would be worth several years in the future. But we were living in the moment, and we cashed it in. At least we used the money to purchase our home, but it was still a huge mistake. We lost a great opportunity and who knows how much money.

Today's Winning Thought: *"Do not wait; the time will never be 'just right.' Start where you stand, and work with whatever tools you may have at your command, and better tools will be found as you go along."* (George Herbert)

Simplify

make easier to understand or master

The older I get, the more interested I am in simplifying my life. I have an unwritten rule that whenever I enter a room in my house, I look for something, perhaps a few things, that I can take out of that room when I leave. I cannot just remove it from the room, I must give it or throw it away. I probably have too much stuff.

Bill Hybels, founding and senior pastor of Willow Creek Community Church in South Barrington Hills, Illinois, wrote a book in 2014 titled *Simplify*. In the book, Hybels outlined ten practices to unclutter your soul and your life. When you simplify your life, he suggests that you will go . . .

From exhausted to energized.

From overscheduled to organized.

From overwhelmed to in control.

From restless to fulfilled.

From wounded to whole.

From anxious to peaceful.

From isolated to connected.

From drifting to focused.

From stuck to moving on.

From meaningless to satisfied.

I am still working on that list. I intend to move from the words on the left side of Hybels's list to the words on the right. It is taking time, but I will accomplish it. It will require focus, being very intentional and determined. I have to change some things in my life and eliminate others.

Today's Winning Thought: Simplify your life.

Society

*group sharing a common culture; location; human
beings in their relations with one another*

We live in a society that is being ripped apart at the seams. I believe there are four things in particular on which we can place the blame.

Drugs.

Illiteracy.

Lack of personal accountability.

Poor personal money management.

Some or all of the issues mentioned above have contributed to another problem, a major one—the breakdown of the family.

Some people have overcome one or more of these problems. If you struggle in any of these areas, get help today. These things will steal your life. Help is available. Get it. Intervene for someone else who needs it.

Today's Winning Thought: One of the greatest needs that exists in America today is the need to break the cycle that is keeping individuals and families in perpetual poverty and dysfunction.

Success

favorable outcome of an attempt; commonly sought goals

Do you want to be successful? You can be. A good first step is to look in the mirror. That is the person you need to start with. Talk to him or her.

Owning the other ninety-nine words in this book will go a long way toward making you successful. They are all important and they all matter. Together, they will all be a factor in your success.

Life will not always be fair. But do not settle for less. Settle for more. Persevere. Remember what Irish poet Oliver Goldsmith once said: "Success consists of getting up just one more time than you fall."

Today's Winning Thought: *"The road to success is filled with the potholes of failure." (Kevin O'Leary)*

Teachable

to be informed on a subject

I decided on this word while mentoring some third-grade students one day. I was reading with a group of six or seven students, many of whom who do not sit still very long, boss each other, and talk at the same time. While returning to their classroom, I mentioned to one of the boys that I know a youngster who tripped on his shoestring one day and fell and broke his leg. I encouraged my little friend to tie his shoestring because I would hate for that to happen to him. Most of the other kids I have suggested that to tie their shoe right away. Not this one. He said he will never fall. And if he did, he could catch himself and break his fall.

I did not remind him that he fell out of his chair twenty minutes earlier because the chair was not on all four legs. I wanted to tell him that he needs to listen to those who are trying to help him. He might even learn something. He might have a rude awakening if he ignores a future coach or boss. Players have been dismissed from teams for that kind of attitude. There is time for him to change. He is only in the third grade.

Third graders are not the only ones who possess the potential to be unteachable. Adults, including some parents, are susceptible to this too.

I saw a Facebook post recently. It showed a sign that was posted in an arena. It was directed at parents of little league hockey players. It read, "Your child's success or lack of success in sports does not indicate what kind of parent you are. But having an athlete that is coachable, respectable, a great teammate, mentally tough, resilient and tries their best IS a direct reflection of your parenting."

I do not know who wrote that sign, but they hit the nail squarely on the head. If you are a parent of a child involved in sports, music, or other activities, I would encourage you to make this a point of emphasis.

Being coachable and teachable will put you in a position to become successful.

It helped Brynn Minor become a better softball player. During her freshman season in college, her coach decided he wanted the first-year player to throw batting practice to give the team's pitchers a break. Minor was recruited because of her hitting. But her coach needed something more. After a few batting practice sessions, her coach realized her teammates could not hit her. Being approachable and coachable led to even greater and immediate success for Minor and her teammates. Her batting average was .486 (exceptionally good). But even more impressive was her 0.60 ERA (Earned Run Average), which was second in the nation. Her success, individual and team, will earn her more attention when she moves from the junior college level to Division 1.

When your coach or boss asks you to make a change to help your team or company, you will also be helping yourself. Make the change without grumbling.

After winning his third world championship, bull rider Tuff Hedeman did not have a big celebration. He moved on to Denver to start a new season and started the whole process all over again. His comment was, "The bull won't care what I did last week."

Whether you are an untested rookie or a veteran and world champion, if you want to be a champion tomorrow, be teachable today.

Today's Winning Thought: Being teachable does not end. Be a life-long learner.

Today

present day

Today is the day you can start over. This day will be your new starting point. Just focus on today. It is all you have. Sir William Osler once advised letting go of dead yesterdays and unborn tomorrows. He said, "The load of tomorrow added to that of yesterday, carried today, makes the strongest falter."

It is wise to learn the lessons from all of your yesterdays, but don't stay there. It is good to plan ahead, to plan for the future. But what you do or fail to do today will have an effect on those plans.

Know this: Life is short, no matter how long you live. And it can be taken away in an instant. We would be wise to remember Psalm 90:12. "Teach us to number our days, that we gain a heart of wisdom." It would behoove us to live more wisely.

Today, think about this: What do you want to see happen in your life before you die? What step will you take toward that purpose today?

Today's Winning Thought: *"Most people don't aim too high and miss; they aim too low and hit." (Bob Moawad)*

Truth

that which is actually so

I am a Rotarian. One of the tenets of Rotary is something known as The Four-Way Test. It is not something to be recited, it is to be practiced. Here is what Rotarians believe.

Of the things we think, say, or do,

Is it the *truth*?

Is it *fair* to all concerned?

Will it build *goodwill* and better friendships?

Will it be *beneficial* to all concerned?

Today's Winning Thought: Those are four questions you should ask yourself and live by. Clearly, the world we live in would be a better place if even a few people subscribed to philosophy of Rotary's Four-Way Test.

Try

make an effort or attempt to do something

My daughter is twenty-six years old. She has Down syndrome. One of the places she volunteers is a school. She spends part of one day each week with some third-grade students. A few years ago, she was also helping a kindergarten teacher. My daughter loves to read. One day, she was reading to a group of students and one of them was not listening. She stopped and told the youngster, "I have Down syndrome and I can read. You need to pay attention and try harder."

In life, you are going to have to put forth some effort, if you expect to succeed. Like my daughter said, you need to pay attention and try harder.

I cannot tell you anything about *Star Wars*. I am not a fan. I would not sit and watch five minutes of it for five dollars. But there is a quote, courtesy of Yoda, that challenges you and me. "Do or do not. There is no try." I cannot tell you with certainty, but my guess is that the phrase is meant to challenge you to succeed. "I will try" could mean you think failure is a real and present possibility. Believe in yourself. Believe that you will be successful.

Don't quit too soon. Thomas Edison said, "Our greatest weakness lies in giving up. The most certain way to succeed is always to try just one more time."

Today's Winning Thought: *"Ever tried. Ever failed. No matter. Try again. Fail again. Fail better."* (Samuel Beckett)

Think

employ the mind

A few years ago, Starbucks rolled out a new product. They introduced VIA Ready Brew, an instant coffee that the company hoped would drive up sales. Some months later, with the new product on its way to stores, Starbucks CEO Howard Schultz asked his team to "think big and then think bigger."

What would happen in homes, schools, businesses, and personal lives if we all thought big and then thought bigger? Ken Blanchard, author of *One-Minute Manager*, said we would astound ourselves. "If you want to go to places you have never been before, you have to think in ways you have never thought before."

Today's Winning Thought: You will take a major gain in your personal growth if you schedule time every day to think. It is vital to your success. Today, start thinking, and then think bigger. And better.

Technology

application of science

I have heard it said that when someone, men in particular, gets angry, it is generally preceded by frustration. More than once, I have been very angry at myself because of my lack of knowledge in the area of technology. This causes me plenty of frustration. It is made worse because I cannot find the help I need.

My point here is not anger or frustration. It is the source of what is causing my stress—technology.

If you are a young person, I could probably have left this word off my list. You have probably forgotten more technology than I will ever know. If you do not have a grasp on technology, learn it well and learn it soon. And learn how to not let it run or ruin your life.

This might not ruin your life, but being careless in the way you communicate will not earn you respect very quickly. Learn to spell and write complete sentences. Texting has created a world of young people who do not write well and who do not converse well. Know how to communicate.

A business manager told me she gave a young employee some envelopes and postcards one day with the different stamps that were to be affixed for mailing. When she got them back, many of them were wrong. Some of the stamps that were supposed to go on the letters were on postcards and some of the lower priced stamps for the postcards were on the letters. The nineteen-year-old employee had put the wrong stamps on several pieces of the mail. When asked about the mistake, she said she did not know there was a difference in the postage. She had never addressed an envelope in her life.

Be better than that young woman. Have a basic understanding of how things work. Show proper etiquette when it comes to your cell phone and electronic devices. And put them down once in a while and have real conversations.

Today's Winning Thought: *"The moment of drifting into thought has been so clipped by modern technology. Our lives are filled with distraction with smartphones and all the rest. People are so locked into not being present."* (Glen Hansard)

Urgency

pressing; vital; crucial

I asked a friend if he would share a word that was important to him. He is a husband and father of two young sons and leads a successful business which employs several people. I was confident that he would have many great words. I asked him because his words would be on the mark. I knew he would also encourage me.

His word was *urgency*. It is vital that we have a sense of urgency. I asked if that was a word he has been sharing with his own boys. He said he has been talking about having a sense of urgency with his employees.

I can really relate with that word. The older I get, the faster life seems to go. I have been trying to live with a sense of urgency. None of us are guaranteed tomorrow. Our lives can end abruptly. Mine could easily have ended in late 2014 when I was involved in an automobile accident.

My first book was at the publisher at the time of the accident. I know I have more to write, and I am really feeling that sense of urgency.

Do not rush through life. Enjoy your life, but live with purpose, live expectantly and abundantly. Someone once said that life is short no matter how long you live.

Today's Winning Thought: Live with a sense of urgency.

Vision

foresight

Andy Stanley, senior pastor of North Point Community Church in Atlanta, Georgia, said a vision is a clear mental picture of what could be, fueled by the conviction that it should be. Stanley wrote a book titled *Visioneering*. He said visioneering is the engineering of a vision.

"A clear vision, along with the courage to follow through, dramatically increase your chances of coming to the end of your life, looking back with a deep abiding satisfaction, and thinking, I did it. I succeeded. I finished well. My life counted."

Without a clear vision, Stanley said the odds are you will come to the end of your life and wonder what you could have done or should have done. You might even wonder if your life mattered at all.

Today's Winning Thought: Do you have a vision? You will know it when it comes to you. When it does, act on it.

Victim

sufferer from a force, or action; dupe

Sometime in your life, you are going to be treated unfairly, be snubbed or rejected. There might be some who even go out of their way to make your life miserable. Do not help them. Rise above it. You are not a victim.

We live in a country divided. Hatred and intolerance run rampant. I believe that many people add fuel to those fires. But I also believe it would be a terrible mistake for you to allow the actions of some to ruin your life. You are responsible for your own life. Get up, get knowledge, get positive, get moving forward—get in control of your life.

There are so many people who have overcome challenges and issues in their life that you could not possibly find the time to read about all of them. They did not overcome and achieve by having a victim mentality.

Today's Winning Thought: Start believing in yourself, and never stop. You are not a victim. Don't act like it, and don't live like it.

Who

which person

My Twitter profile describes me like this:

Husband, dad, and business guy who helps people recognize and reward others. Also fighting the battle against illiteracy. It is a war that must be won.

It stopped there. It did not include something else that is very important to me: my faith in God. Also missing from my Twitter profile is my passion for helping individuals and families be good managers of their money and resources.

That is who I am. Who are you? What is your passion? What burdens you? What are you doing about it? What might not get started or completed if you do not get involved?

You do not need a title to be a leader. You do not need to have authority to help people. You do not need to be a millionaire to serve others. You just need to act.

Today's Winning Thought: *"You are successful. Will you choose to matter?" (Seth Godin)*

Wisdom

knowledge and good judgment; wise teachings

This might be one of the most important words in this book. It is primary and fundamental. I believe that wisdom is the foundation on which life is built.

If someone offered you the most prestigious degree you could receive, the nicest home you could build and any amount of money you would request or wisdom, it should be a no-brainer. Choose wisdom—*every* time.

The battle for wisdom is never over. "Get understanding" might imply that you need to go after it. Seek wisdom. Embrace it. It leads to peace and life.

Today's Winning Thought: *"Though it costs you all you have, get understanding." (Proverbs 4:7)*

Write

form letters or words

Get some command of the English language. Don't try to impress people with big words that you do not know the meaning of. Know your words, and use them properly. And spell them correctly when you write. You might consider making a dictionary your best friend.

You are going to spend many hours speaking to people and many more hours corresponding via e-mail. Mistakes will happen. Just keep them to a minimum. You can, and should, think before you speak. When you write, you can proof your work before hitting Send. Do not get in a big hurry. Pausing long enough to proofread what I was preparing to send saved me from sending what would have been a very embarrassing e-mail.

I was writing an e-mail to a female recipient one day. I was informing her that another female who we were planning to meet with was busy and would be unable to meet. If you will notice on your keyboard, the letter immediately left of the letter *Y* is the letter *T*. I had, obviously unintentionally, hit the *T* before typing the *Y*. Now all of the sudden, this lady was too busty to meet with us. Do you know how thankful I was to have caught that error before I hit Send? Be careful. Double-check your work.

Today's Winning Thought: Learn to write well. Be concise. And do not forget that spelling words correctly is important.

Work

labor or toil

Success always comes before work—in the dictionary.

I did not always work hard when I was a young man. That changed the day I was told that I might not graduate from high school. I wanted the passing grade, but I did not want to do the work that was required.

It was about that time that I was beginning a career in broadcasting. I applied myself to that, and I worked diligently. I cared about that. I did not care about school.

If you want to experience success in life, have a strong work ethic.

The Bible goes so far as to say if a man is unwilling to work he should not eat (2 Thessalonians 3:10).

This is a great definition, courtesy of Ashton Kutcher:

"I believe that opportunity looks a lot like work. When I was 13 I had my first job with dad carrying shingles to the roof, and then I got a job washing dishes at a restaurant, and then I got a job in a grocery store deli, and then I got a job in a factory sweeping Cheerio dust off the ground. And I never had a job in my life that I was better than. I was always just lucky to have a job. And every job I had was a stepping stone to my next job. And I never quit my job until I had my next job. So, opportunity looks a lot like work."

I had two jobs in high school that I really did not appreciate as much as I should have. One of them was a summer job at a flour mill. The other was the all-night shift at a potato chip factory.

Charles Koch is the chairman of the board and CEO of Koch Industries, Inc., the second largest private company in the United States. He wrote about the importance and value of work in his book

Good Profit. "Don't underestimate the value of the work experience you have as a teenager and young adult."

Today's Winning Thought: Opportunity is often disguised as work.

Worry

feel anxious; make anxious; anxiety

Here are some things I have heard about worry.

"Our fatigue is often caused not by work, but by worry, frustration and resentment." (Dale Carnegie)

"Worry does not empty tomorrow of its sorrows. It empties today of its strengths." (Corrie Ten Boom)

"Worry is the stomach's worst poison." (Alfred Nobel)

"When you begin to worry, go find something to do. Get busy being a blessing to someone; do something fruitful. Talking about your problem or sitting alone, thinking about it, does no good; it serves only to make you miserable. Above all else, remember that worrying is totally useless. Worrying will not solve your problem." (Joyce Meyer)

Today's Winning Thought: Do you get the idea that worrying is about as useful as two dead flies? Worrying will get you nowhere fast.

Waste

use up needlessly; ruin

I wish I had half the minutes I have wasted in my life. I wish I had half the money I have wasted on things I did not need. I wish I had not wasted the early years of my life when I could have started saving money sooner.

I have wasted too many minutes, hours, days, and heartbeats. Opportunities I will not get back. Do not waste heartbeats. Take care of the minutes. You will not get them back.

Today's Winning Thought: The late Steve Jobs once said, "Your time is limited, so don't waste it living someone else's life. Don't be trapped by dogma, which is living with the results of other people's thinking. Don't let the noise of other's opinions drown out your own inner voice. And most important, have the courage to follow your heart and intuition. They somehow already know what you truly want to become. Everything else is secondary."

You

person or persons addressed; any person

Imagine that you have just accepted a new position as chairman and chief executive officer of You, Inc. What would be your first order of business?

That really is not too far-fetched. You are the person—the only person—in charge of your life and your new company. And your new job begins today. How will you lead your company and yourself? Do you have a plan and a strategy? You cannot lead it successfully without an idea of where you want to go and who you want to be. As S. L. Parker, author of *212: The Extra Degree*, wrote, "It's your life. You are responsible for your results. It is time to turn up the heat."

The late Zig Ziglar said, "If you don't like who you are and where you are, don't worry about it because you are not stuck with who you are or where you are. You can grow. You can change. You can be more than you are."

Today's Winning Thought: *"Hold yourself to a higher standard."* *(Henry Ward Beacher)*

ZAP

to attack, defeat, or destroy with sudden speed and force

The leaders of a small Kansas school district developed a plan recently that is literally changing the lives of many of their students. They call the program ZAP. It stands for Zeros Aren't Permitted. They are simply not going to allow students to get a zero on an assignment. You get a zero when you fail to complete and turn in a class assignment. Enough zeros will result in the student receiving an F for that class.

Basically, this program forces students to complete assignments. They stay after school to finish their work. If they miss a school bus, their parents or someone will come after them. And the best grade they can make on the assignment they are finishing is 75 percent.

The idea is to prevent these students from failing. And it seems to be working very well. A recent week showed only one student with an F. It is teaching self-discipline and personal accountability, which the students will need when they enter the workforce. Those are characteristics of successful people.

Too many students do just barely enough to get a passing grade. I thought a D was fine because it is technically a passing grade. Those students really exist. I was one of them more than 40 years ago. I played to keep from losing, instead of playing to win. Playing to keep from losing is no way to live. Not for your students, if you are a parent of school-aged children, and certainly not for yourself if you are in the work force.

Today's Winning Thought: Zeros Aren't Permitted, or a similar program, should be considered by every school in America.

A Final Thought

Don't expect anyone to widen the plate for you. Here is what I mean.

Maybe you have read or heard this story. If not, you need to. If so, it is worth reading again.

John Scolinos was a college baseball coach. He coached at Pepperdine University and Cal Poly Pomona University and also served as the pitching coach Team USA in the 1984 Olympics. He retired with 1,198 wins and three national championships. So I guess he had credentials and knew what he was talking about.

One day, he was speaking to a large group of coaches at a convention. At seventy-eight years old, he slowly shuffled to the podium wearing a home plate around his neck. He spoke for several minutes and finally mentioned his necklace. He asked if there were any little league coaches in attendance. There were. He asked, "How wide is home plate?"

The coaches replied that it is seventeen inches. He also recognized high school coaches, college coaches, and those who worked at the professional level. He asked the same question of the other coaches. All replied correctly. Home plate is seventeen inches wide at every level you play, from Little League to the major leagues.

Then it got real.

"Do you know what they do with a major leaguer who cannot throw the ball over the seventeen-inch plate?" the retired coach asked. "They send him to the minors. They don't say, 'Ah, that's okay, Jimmy. You can't hit seventeen inches, so we'll make it eighteen or nineteen or twenty inches."

The old coach said to the crowd that had now gone silent, "Do we hold people accountable or do we change the rules to fit them? Do we widen the plate?"

He said society does not teach accountability. There are no consequences for failing to meet standards. We have widened the plate. And if we continue, there are dark days ahead.

Coach Scolinos's remarks before the turn of the century were profound. Look at where widening the plate has gotten us. I believe in grace and second chances. I have been on the receiving end of both. I also believe it is important to fail. Some lessons cannot be learned any other way.

You have some control in determining how successful you will become. John Addison, the former co-CEO of Primerica, and the author of *Real Leadership: 9 Simple Practices for Leading and Living With Purpose*, said, "Your destiny is your decision." Addison added that although there are some things you cannot control, you can control who you are and how you respond to challenges.

I want you to win in life. But don't focus on winning, focus on the process. Do the right things, for the right reasons, all the time. Do these basic things really well and you put yourself in a lot better position to win.

I want you to take one minute and write down your takeaway from what you have just read. Then, keep that paper where you will see it often. Let it serve as a reminder to you. Give careful thought to the words in this book. Don't borrow them—*own* them.

Is there a word, or words, that you will take away from this book and own?

What Others Say

"Marv Loucks approaches his life with his sight words in front of him on a daily basis. He speaks from his heart, believes what he writes, and lives with the belief that successful people keep what is important at the forefront of every decision he makes as a businessman, husband and a father." (John Blazek, Retired School Administrator/GM/Coach/Referee)

"Anyone involved in the development of a child should start with Sight Words. *A spot-on set of words that guide and teach on what to reinforce in a child so they can grow into a whole, grounded person that possesses wisdom, grace and virtues." (Jean Ann Hankins, Executive Director, Ronald McDonald House Charities of Tulsa, Oklahoma)*

"Words have remarkable power. In Sight Words, *author Marv Loucks make clear that it's not just any words. There are certain words you will never want to let out of your sight. 100 such words are offered on these pages. But it's owning and living these words that matters, the author contends. To help readers do that, this book is chock-full of inspiring quotes and stories, helpful applications, as well as words that warn, encourage, admonish, give hope and guidance. Each word has a definition, a few sentences explaining how that word could impact your life and a summary thought so you can win by owning it.* Sight Words *can be read in a single evening, or take one word each days and let it soak in. It proposes 100 words that can take you to a new level." (Rev. Dr. Randy J. Gauger)*

"In the more than 30 years that I have known Marv, the way he uses his words and the way he writes always have had the power to influence and inspire. What I value most about him is that Marv actually LIVES the words he writes about in here. However, I think he forgot a cou-

ple. ELOQUENCE—Marv's writing is true eloquence. HONESTY—Marv's actions and life are pure honesty. This is a great reminder of the power of the words we use to harm and to heal." (Kimera Way, President, University of Wisconsin-Eau Claire Foundation)

"Everyday words take on new, empowering meanings in Sight Words. *Marv challenges us all to look beyond simple definitions to better understand the influence we have to make life better for ourselves and others. This book is packed with inspiration from A to Z." (Katie Grover, SVP, Marketing Director, Fidelity Bank | Oklahoma Fidelity Bank)*

"In his book, Sight Words, *Marv has captured the essence and importance of individual words. Words have consequences, some positive and some negative. Because of the interpretation of one word, annual challenges have been made before the Kansas Supreme Court on Kansas School Finance Law. That one word was in a constitutional amendment that was passed 24 years previously. Words, used appropriately, can have a great positive effect on our personal relationships, our business, professional and political lives. Marv has helped us to properly use and enjoy the use of words. Thanks, Marv, by reminding us of their importance, you have added to our ability to communicate. Your words have not fallen on deaf ears. You have helped many to a better understanding and appreciation of the words used every day and have enriched our lives. My prayer is that* Sight Words *will be a great blessing to all who will read it." (Bill Mason, Retired Business Executive and State Legislator)*

"In an era where my generation has limited its attention span to 140 characters, Sight Words *manages to condense decades of wisdom into just 100 salient terms. Marv Loucks provides a comprehensive, yet simple playbook for success, happiness, and problem solving. Millennials in particular can utilize* Sight Words *as a Rosetta Stone to navigate our*

increasingly chaotic and challenging world." (Christian B. Corrigan, Constitutional Litigation Fellow, Institute for Justice)

"Marv Loucks speaks with the wisdom of a father, a business owner, and a gentleman. As I read his narrative on 100 important words, I had flashbacks to my own father's advice (BOLD: "Don't expect something for nothing."), advice I've received from mentors (INTEGRITY: "Have the courage to face the truth."), and pastors (SERVE: "Put others before yourself."). His recommendations under READ will occupy my weekends for the next year or more. In short, Marv's compilation of these 100 words is a book every leader should give to their followers and keep on their own bedside table for late-night inspiration and guidance." (Dr. J. Bradford G. Hodson, Executive Vice-President Development, Missouri Southern State University, Joplin, Missouri)

Sometimes, life can be as simple as focusing on the power of words. Words can heal as easily as they can harm. Words can open doors, or have those doors slammed in our face. Words can persuade an argument or discourage further consideration. Our choice of words defines us as they reveal our character, our world view, our passions, our experiences, our beliefs and ultimately these words informs our behavior in the manner in which we treat others, and meet life's challenges.

In this book, Marv Loucks provides his unique perspective on everyday words that will allow the reader to reflect on the message he presents with 100 of his favorite words. Communication, whether verbal or written, is part of our daily opportunity to convey what's in our hearts, and in our minds. Own your words, and you'll own the conversation. (Markus K. Scholler, VP, Freddy's LLC).

About the Author

Marv Loucks is a businessman and writer. He is also a retired college basketball official and the founder of Vision 2020, a task force in his community, whose mission is the fight against illiteracy. He writes a daily blog, With Regard to Life, which can be found at marvloucks.com. Marv lives in El Dorado, Kansas, with his wife, Kerri, and daughter, Kyle.

CPSIA information can be obtained
at www.ICGtesting.com
Printed in the USA
FFOW03n2258190518
46724636-48851FF